Y0-AUD-743

GREAT WORDS OF JESUS

Thomas Nelson Publishers
Nashville • Camden • New York

GOOD NEWS FOR THE POOR

Jesus went to Nazareth,...and on the Sabbath he went as usual to the synagogue. He stood up to read the Scriptures and was handed the book of the prophet Isaiah. He unrolled the scroll and found the place where it is written, "The Spirit of the Lord is upon me, because he has chosen me to bring good news to the poor. He has sent me to proclaim liberty to the captives and recovery of sight to the blind, to set free the oppressed and announce that the time has come when the Lord will save his people."

Jesus rolled up the scroll, gave it back to the attendant, and sat down. All the people in the synagogue had their eyes fixed on him, as he said to them, "This passage of scripture has come true today, as you heard it being read."

LUKE 4:16-21

For peasant farmers, poverty is a factor of life.

TAKE MY YOKE

Jesus said, "Come to me, all of you who are tired from carrying heavy loads, and I will give you rest. Take my yoke and put it on you, and learn from me, because I am gentle and humble in spirit; and you will find rest. For the yoke I will give you is easy, and the load I will put on you is light."

MATTHEW 11:28-30

HEAR ME

Anyone who comes to me and listens to my words and obeys them—I will show you what he is like. He is like a man who, in building his house, dug deep and laid the foundation on rock. The river flooded over and hit the house but could not shake

Conversation piece beneath the walls of Jerusalem.

it, because it was well built. But anyone who hears my words and does not obey them is like a man who built his house without laying a foundation; when the flood hit that house it fell at once—and what a terrible crash that was!

LUKE 6:47–49

FINDING LIFE

Jesus called the crowd and his disciples to him. "If anyone wants to come with me," he told them, "he must forget himself, carry his cross, and follow me. For whoever wants to save his own life will lose it; but whoever loses his life for me and for the gospel will save it. Does a person gain anything if he wins the whole world but loses his life? Of course not! There is nothing he can give to regain his life."

MARK 8:34-37

Giant poppies reach toward the sun.

THE BREAD OF LIFE

Jesus said..."It is my Father who gives you the real bread from heaven. For the bread that God gives is he who comes down from heaven and gives life to the world."

"Sir," they asked him, "give us this bread always."

"I am the bread of life," Jesus told them. "He who comes to me will never be hungry; he who believes in me will never be thirsty."

"I will never turn away anyone who comes to me."

JOHN 6:32–35, 37

Flat loaves of bread.

THE LIGHT OF THE WORLD

Jesus spoke to the Pharisees...."I am the light of the world," he said. "Whoever follows me will have the light of life and will never walk in darkness."

JOHN 8:12

Dawn in the Dardanelles.

THE GATE FOR THE SHEEP

Jesus said again, "I am telling you the truth: I am the gate for the sheep. All others who came before me are thieves and robbers, but the sheep did not listen to them. I am the gate. Whoever comes in by me will be saved; he will come in and go out and find pasture. The thief comes only in order to steal, kill, and destroy. I have come in order that you might have life—life in all its fullness."

JOHN 10:7–10

The shepherd's flock seek out the shade on the terraced hillsides of Israel.

THE WAY

On the evening before his death, Jesus said to his disciples:

"I am going to prepare a place for you. I would not tell you this if it were not so. And after I go and prepare a place for you, I will come back and take you to myself, so that you will be where I am. You know the way that leads to the place where I am going."

Thomas said to him, "Lord, we do not know where you are going; so how can we know the way to get there?"

Jesus answered him, "I am the way, the truth, and the life; no one goes to the Father except by me."

JOHN 14:2–6

Stone steps mark the way in Israel.

THE GOOD SHEPHERD

I am the good shepherd, who is willing to die for the sheep. When the hired man, who is not a shepherd and does not own the sheep, sees a wolf coming, he leaves the sheep and runs away; so the wolf snatches the sheep and scatters them. The hired man runs away because he is only a hired man and does not care about the sheep.

I am the good shepherd. As the Father knows me and I know the Father, in the same way I know my sheep and they know me. And I am willing to die for them.

JOHN 10:11–15

A shepherd with his flock among the olive trees in Israel.

THE VINE

I am the real vine, and my Father is the gardener. He breaks off every branch in me that does not bear fruit, and he prunes every branch that does bear fruit so that it will be clean and bear more fruit. You have been made clean already by the teaching I have given you. Remain united to me, and I will remain united to you. A branch cannot bear fruit by itself; it can do so only if it remains in the vine. In the same way you cannot bear fruit unless you remain in me.

JOHN 15:1–4

Branches are pruned to improve the yield of the vine.

THE RESURRECTION AND THE LIFE

Martha said to Jesus, "If you had been here, Lord, my brother would not have died! But I know that even now God will give you whatever you ask him for."

"Your brother will rise to life," Jesus told her.

"I know," she replied, "that he will rise to life on the last day."

Jesus said to her, "I am the resurrection and the life. Whoever believes in me will live, even though he dies; and whoever lives and believes in me will never die. Do you believe this?"

JOHN 11:21-26

The traditional site of Lazarus's tomb at Bethany.

HIDDEN TREASURE

The Kingdom of heaven is like this. A man happens to find a treasure hidden in a field. He covers it up again, and is so happy that he goes and sells everything he has, and then goes back and buys that field.

Also, the Kingdom of heaven is like this. A man is looking for fine pearls, and when he finds one that is unusually fine, he goes and sells everything he has, and buys that pearl.

MATTHEW 13:44–46

A NEW BIRTH

A Jewish leader called Nicodemus came to Jesus with questions:

Jesus answered: "I am telling you the truth, no one can see the Kingdom of God unless he is born again." "How can a grown man be born again?" Nicodemus asked. "He certainly cannot enter his mother's womb and be born a second time!" "I am telling you the truth," replied Jesus, "that no one can enter the Kingdom of God unless he is born of water and the Spirit. A person is born physically of human parents, but he is born spiritually of the Spirit. Do not be surprised because I tell you that you must all be born again."

"As Moses lifted up the bronze snake on a pole in the desert, in the same way the Son of Man must be lifted up, so that everyone who believes in him may have eternal life. For God loved the world so much that he gave his only Son, so that everyone who believes in him may not die but have eternal life."

JOHN 3:3–7, 14–16

A sparkling stream in Galilee.

THE PEOPLE OF THE KINGDOM

Happy are those who know they are spiritually poor;
the Kingdom of heaven belongs to them!
Happy are those who mourn;
God will comfort them!
Happy are those who are humble;
they will receive what God has promised!
Happy are those whose greatest desire is to do what God requires;
God will satisfy them fully!
Happy are those who are merciful to others;
God will be merciful to them!
Happy are the pure in heart;
they will see God!
Happy are those who work for peace;
God will call them his children!

MATTHEW 5:3-9

LOVE YOUR ENEMIES

You have heard that it was said, "Love your friends, hate your enemies." But now I tell you: love your enemies and pray for those who persecute you, so that you may become the sons of your Father in heaven.

MATTHEW 5:43–45

Conversation in a street in Aleppo, Syria.

DON'T CONDEMN—FORGIVE

Do not judge others, and God will not judge you; do not condemn others, and God will not condemn you; forgive others, and God will forgive you. Give to others, and God will give to you. Indeed, you will receive a full measure, a generous helping, poured into your hands—all that you can hold. The measure you use for others is the one that God will use for you.

LUKE 6:37-38

Goods are weighed and measured in the market at Bethlehem.

LIGHT FOR THE WORLD

You are like light for the whole world. A city built on a hill cannot be hid. No one lights a lamp and puts in under a bowl; instead he puts it on the lampstand, where it gives light for everyone in the house.

In the same way your light must shine before people, so that they will see the good things you do and praise your Father in heaven.

MATTHEW 5:14–16

Oil lamps modeled on those in use in Bible times burn with a steady flame.

RICHES IN HEAVEN

Do not store up riches for yourselves here on earth, where moths and rust destroy, and robbers break in and steal.

Instead, store up riches for yourselves in heaven, where moths and rust cannot destroy, and robbers cannot break in and steal. For your heart will always be where your riches are.

MATTHEW 6:19–21

Gold drinking vessels from ancient Persia.

A LESSON IN HOW TO PRAY

One day Jesus was praying in a certain place. When he had finished, one of his disciples said to him, "Lord, teach us to pray, just as John taught his disciples."

Ripe ears of wheat to be turned into bread for a hungry world.

"When you pray, say this:
'Father: May your holy name be honored; may your Kingdom come. Give us day by day the food we need. Forgive us our sins, for we forgive everyone who does us wrong. And do not bring us to hard testing.'"

LUKE 11:1-4

SEARCHING AND FINDING

Ask, and you will receive; seek, and you will find; knock, and the door will be opened to you. For everyone who asks will receive, and anyone who seeks will find, and the door will be opened to him who knocks.

Would any of you who are fathers give your son a stone when he asks for bread? Or would you give him a snake when he asks for a fish? As bad as you are, you know how to give good things to your children. How much more, then, will your Father in heaven give good things to those who ask him!

MATTHEW 7:7–11

Doors to the quaint cone-shaped dwellings of Cappadocia (Turkey).

THE CHOICE

No one can be a slave of two masters; he will hate one and love the other; he will be loyal to one and despise the other. You cannot serve both God and money.

MATTHEW 6:24

Roman coins showing the heads of emperors Tiberius and Claudius, from New Testament times.

SERVING OTHERS

The men who are considered rulers of the heathen have power over them, and the leaders have complete authority. This, however, is not the way it is among you. If one of you wants to be great, he must be the servant of the rest; and if one of you wants to be first, he must be the slave of all. For even the Son of Man did not come to be served; he came to serve and to give his life to redeem many people.

MARK 10:42–45

From ancient times to the present day donkeys have been man's beasts of burden.

LOVE YOUR NEIGHBOR

A teacher of the Law asked Jesus,

"Which is the greatest commandment in the Law?" Jesus answered, " 'Love the Lord your God with all your heart, with all your soul, and with all your mind.' This is the greatest and the most important commandment. The second most important commandment is like it: 'Love your neighbor as you love yourself.' "

MATTHEW 22:35–39

Women work together to gather in the harvest.

LIKE CHILDREN

The disciples came to Jesus, asking, "Who is the greatest in the Kingdom of heaven?"

So Jesus called a child, had him stand in front of them, and said, "I assure you that unless you change and become like children, you will never enter the Kingdom of heaven. The greatest in the Kingdom of heaven is the one who humbles himself and becomes like this child. And whoever welcomes in my name one such child as this, welcomes me."

MATTHEW 18:1–5

Two Bedouin children from Jordan.

GOD WILL PROVIDE

It is God who clothes the wild grass—grass that is here today and gone tomorrow, burned up in the oven. Won't he be all the more sure to clothe you? What little faith you have!
So do not start worrying: "Where will my food come from? or my drink? or my clothes?" (These are the things the pagans are always concerned about.) Your Father in heaven knows that you need all these things.

Instead, be concerned above everything else with the Kingdom of God and with what he requires of you, and he will provide you with all these other things.

So do not worry about tomorrow; it will have enough worries of its own. There is no need to add to the troubles each day brings.

MATTHEW 6:30–34

Flowers of Galilee.

THE PROMISE OF FREEDOM

Jesus said to those who believed in him, "If you obey my teaching, you are really my disciples; you will know the truth, and the truth will set you free."

"We are the descendants of Abraham," they answered, "and we have never been anybody's slaves. What do you mean, then, by saying, 'You will be free'?"

Jesus said to them, "I am telling you the truth: everyone who sins is a slave of sin. A slave does not belong to a family permanently, but a son belongs there for ever. If the Son sets you free, then you will be really free."

JOHN 8:31–36

ETERNAL LIFE

I am telling you the truth: whoever hears my words and believes in him who sent me has eternal life. He will not be judged, but has already passed from death to life.

JOHN 5:24

WELCOME AND REWARD

Whoever welcomes you welcomes me; and whoever welcomes me welcomes the one who sent me. Whoever welcomes God's messenger because he is God's messenger, will share in his reward. And whoever welcomes a good man because he is good, will share in his reward.

You can be sure that whoever gives even a drink of cold water to one of the least of these my followers because he is my follower, will certainly receive a reward.

MATTHEW 10:40-42

A boy on a donkey passes through the Lion Gate, Jerusalem.

ANSWERED PRAYER

Whenever two of you on earth agree about anything you pray for, it will be done for you by my Father in heaven.

For where two or three come together in my name, I am there with them.

MATTHEW 18:19–20

LAST PROMISES

When I go, you will not be left all alone; I will come back to you. In a little while the world will see me no more, but you will see me; and because I live, you also will live.

I have told you this while I am still with you. The Helper, the Holy Spirit, whom the Father will send in my name, will teach you everything and make you remember all that I have told you.

Peace is what I leave with you; it is my own peace that I give you. I do not give it as the world does. Do not be worried and upset; do not be afraid. You heard me say to you, "I am leaving, but I will come back to you."

JOHN 14:18–19, 25–28

Boat on Lake Galilee.

I WILL BE WITH YOU ALWAYS

After Jesus' death and resurrection:

The eleven disciples went to the hill in Galilee where Jesus had told them to go. When they saw him, they worshiped him, even though some of them doubted.

Jesus drew near and said to them, "I have been given authority in heaven and on earth. Go, then, to all peoples everywhere and make them my disciples: baptize them in the name of the Father, the Son, and the Holy Spirit, and teach them to obey everything I have commanded you. And I will be with you always, to the end of the age."

MATTHEW 28:16–20

Sheep and shepherd on a coast road in Tunisia at sunset.

Original edition published in English under the title
GREAT WORDS OF JESUS by Lion Publishing, Tring,
England, copyright © 1979 Lion Publishing.

First published in the United States and Canada in 1984
by Thomas Nelson Publishers.

All rights reserved. Written permission must be secured
from the publisher to use or reproduce any part of this
book, except for brief quotations in critical reviews or
articles.

Published in Nashville, Tennessee, by Thomas Nelson,
Inc. and distributed in Canada by Lawson Falle, Ltd.,
Cambridge, Ontario.

Photographs by Peter Baker Photographs: page 53 and
endpapers; J. Allan Cash: page 45; Fritz Fankhauser:
pages 7, 17, 19, 51, 55, 57, 59; Sonia Halliday
Photographs: F. H. C. Birch, pages 9, 24, 39, Sonia
Halliday, pages 5, 13, 41, 47, 63, Jane Taylor, pages 29,
31, 49; Heather James: page 61; Lion Publishing/ David
Alexander: pages 1, 11, 21, 27, 33, 35, 37, 43; Middle
East Photographic Archive: page 23; Rex Features: page 3,
15.

Scripture quotations are from the *Good News Bible*—Old
Testament: Copyright © American Bible Society 1976;
New Testament: Copyright © American Bible Society
1966, 1971, 1976.

Printed in Shenzhen, China

ISBN 0-8407-5397-7